Reframe: unlearning false narratives

RaeKenya Walker

BookLeaf Publishing

India | USA | UK

Presentation by *BookLeaf Publishing*

Web: www.bookleafpub.com

E-mail: info@bookleafpub.com

ISBN; 9789363305977
First edition 2024

Antici….pation

Waiting, longing, believing.
With a full heart and wide eyes
I anxiously await my next phase—
The phase where thoughts, feelings, and actions
align.
Leaving old wounds behind
to prepare for a new chapter, a 2nd chance.
Finally feeling whole, for the 1st time in a long
time.
Remembering that this is what happiness feels
like
Head in the clouds, heart on my sleeve but
Trusting the process.
God/Jah/Universe/Spirit/Creator reminding me
to
"Be still and know"
I do know.
I know that:
Being still doesn't equal stagnant.
I know that:
I am whole, even in the waiting
I know that:
Dreams realized are just beyond the horizon.
On the other side of fear,
On the other side of heartbreak…

afterglow

Laying here,
In the still quiet.
The glow of my candle outlines the shape of a
masterpiece.
Respectfully.
Just being.
Hearing your breath and feeling your heartbeat.
I wonder what you're thinking? …. feeling?
Absent minds and full hearts,
Drunk off your scent and your preoccupation
with me.
Not just the lust for my curves but the love of
my brain.
Every inch of me tingles at the thought of…
Heightened senses,
sweet honeysuckle kisses, and deep sighs as the
night comes to an end.
I don't want this to end,
I want to stop time and bask in your afterglow.

Hustle

Girl…. Stop.
You don't have to work yourself to death
anymore.
Our Ancestors worked hard, so you could rest.
Girl… go sit down somewhere.
There is productivity in purposefully slowing
down.
You're not bored, you're just uncomfortable.
Stillness is not complacency but rest is an act of
resistance.
What did you say?
Imposture, where?
Don't let internalized racism and yt supremacy
make you feel like you don't deserve to be here.
Black woman, you are the smartest in the room!
So apply all the pressure.
Black girl, you are enough.
Not too much,
Not minimal or finite,
Enough.
Your strength comes from your ancestors, your
God, your light.
Not the Hustle culture or superwoman narrative.
Yes, we can do it all,
But we don't have to.

Be in your soft life era.
Not weak, but rejoicing in you and all that
you've accomplished.
Your existence alone makes your ancestors
proud and the devil tremble.
Take your mental health day.
Because they want you to break.
Fuck a glass ceiling,
We break molds, necks, and generational curses,
smashing patriarchies and looking fly af while
doing it.
Don't let momma, grandmama, or big mama
project onto you.
They didn't know better, but now we do.
Queen! Adjust your crown.
Smile if you want, or don't.
Just don't carry the world on your shoulders.
No need to Hustle for anyone but yourself
Hustle to lean into you.
To love you,
To honor you.
Hustle, hustle, real hard.

A lesson in grief: You and Taylor aren't the only tortured poets

Stay.

The word dare not leave my lips as you give me back my key.

Can we press pause?

Somebody told me that if you forgive you can forget.

I can't forgive or forget but I can tolerate it.

Broken records, broken hearts. Broken silence.

What happened to you being different?

The only exception to my unlovable troupe?

Hmm, just like everyone else.

You play games if you want.

This queen is making moves;

so, make sure you talk to me nicely.

I'm somebody's future wifey.

You say if I have something to say, I should say
it?!
Don't hurt yourself!
Crazy begets crazy, and I'm a petty bitch.
Talk is cheap,
but you can get this smoke for free.
I can speak for myself, I need no help, no false
allies.
We didn't even need to do all this.
I wanted to be enough for you—
added to your most wanted list.
To be loved by, be seen by you.
Scars, bruises, baggage, and joy.
But I can't have nice things,
you've turned me into a tyrant,
unabashedly taking what's mine!
what I deserve.
Pray for me!
When I become conceited and remember
who I am,
you really won't like me then.
(and then it's over for you hoes)

Thought we could be friends, but you
couldn't even be honest about that.
Unclear expectations lead to
misinterpretation.
I swear, I tried.
Don't tell me I didn't make sacrifices for you,
that I didn't fight for you.
Missed Sunday dinners and conversations made
short because you were in the room.
You didn't have to be my bestie or the love of
my life to see all of me.
We want the same thing.
The thing you're fighting for is everything
I wanted,
but you couldn't,
no, you wouldn't listen.
I'm not a serious person,
but I loved you, seriously.
All I wanted was you.
The anxiety of being too much and not enough
is exhausting.
Society tells me my existence is problematic
and now I feel that at work and at home!
Sorry, my existence causes turmoil for you.
Join the club.
I hate it here.

What was I made for?
not for your entertainment, that's for damn sure!
and not to be played with.

Maybe next time would have been different.

Maybe the 3rd time would have been a charm?

You loved me, but only for a fortnight.

But then it stopped being convenient for you.

I came back to myself, and you couldn't

handle that version of me.

So, I fade back to black, puns, and Freudian

slips intended.

Trauma bonds and misguided ghosts don't leave
much room for true love,

just optics.

Misery loves company but my calendar is full.
So go ahead.
Free yourself.
But be forewarned, the truth hurts.
To know I am 100%
whole, good, and that bitch,

Without you!
2 hands 2 heaven at 3:15 when the music starts
to sound like love again,
self-love for the 1st time. Sweet creature,

This part of the world is brand new.
Ancestors and legacies float above and
cheer us on.
I have to water me 1st,
'cause I've always had me & always will.
I might be too much for you,
but I'm more than enough for me.
Scars, bruises, baggage, and joy.

Dammit Janet

Take up space.
What the hell does that even mean?
Pop culture hashtags and social media handles
reflect my paradoxical being
Social anxiety;
hiding behind medicated confidence-
Sertraline courage and Adderall bravery?
Shadows of perceptions and unclear
expectations consume me.
I want to disappear…
But Take up space.
Be unbossed and unbothered,
Be grounded and firm in who you are
Unapologetically….
Large? Squishy? Expansive?
The proclamation "Don't apologize; it's your job
to take up space" stuck in my throat chakra.
Dammit Janet, you got me.
If I'm gonna be in this bigger body, I might as
well take up space.
It means my heart is so big it needs extra room.
My brain needs more space to do educates,
And that belly laugh that echoes the immense
joy I can feel has to come from somewhere,
right?

You are revolutionary,
Your love, your heart, your mind, and yes your
body.
The audacity you have to Keep. Showing. Up.
There's more room so you can take some of the
weight of the world.
Your hips were made for dancing, they will clear
space for you.
Big hair, don't care,
the coils want to come out and play.
Being perceived is excruciating,
but so is living a lie.
Neurodivergent fairy tales-
talking in circles, hoping someone gets it.
My lizard brain says:
"Don't take it personal, watch your tone, keep
your mouth shut, let your boundaries waver.
You can be a challenge, but not too much,
don't show anger, don't be their stereotype…
Don't run them away, again
But go take up space."
Ok, but if I take up space,
Who will hold space for all of me?
I can not imagine how we begin to forgive
ourselves for all the things we didn't say
until it was too late.
How do we forgive ourselves for all the things
we did not become?
Take up space;

Why are you so lazy?

Why are you so lazy?
Taking a nap right after school
Don't you have homework or better things to do?
Why are you so lazy,
Lying around all-day
I thought you had a great work ethic or at least
some bills to pay.
Why are you so lazy,
not wanting to leave your house
Do you want to be alone forever?
How do you expect to find a spouse?
I never knew you were so lazy,
I thought you had it all together.
But now I see your moods change like East
Tennessee weather.
Have you always been this lazy?
Do you even clean?
I could never live that way, oh, I'm not trying to
be mean.
I expected more from you with all your degrees
and travel,
I can't believe you've been lying,
It looks like your stories are beginning to
unravel.

Well, thanks for the unsolicited advice but
No, I'm not lazy.
School is overstimulating,
I need to rest so my brain can stop
overcompensating.
I do have bills to pay, so I go to work.
But the crippling anxiety is getting worse and
worse.
I hate leaving my house,
outside there are so many things unknown.
Will I fit in the chairs or move through the
stares,
so social outings, I tend to postpone.
I'm not lazy and I don't have it all together
Whoever said that,
bless their hearts, doesn't know any better.
I do my best to mask my fear but it can become
too much and irritability appears.
As far as cleaning goes, I'm not going to lie
I can never meet your expectations, so why even
try?
The executive dysfunction makes cleaning
tough.
It can be paralyzing and I question why I have
so much stuff
Ah, yes degrees and travel!
I've surely been blessed
But this lazy narrative has got me stressed.

Believe it or not, my ADHD, PTSD, and anxiety
don't care,
They don't need an invitation, they show up
anywhere.
Yes, I have the diagnosis to prove it
but I'm also a therapist.
I know,
you'd think the hundred thousand dollars in
student loan debt would take care of this.
Don't forget being Black and Fat in America.
That's a whole other story, right now
Executive dysfunction gets all the glory.
It's hard to be what everyone wants me to be,
Expectations and perceptions get the best of me
I have coping skills I use on a daily,
but since you lack empathy,
you call it being lazy.

Never Be

I don't want to be what you expect of me
my sense of self has faded
longing to be something I am not has left me
jaded
I am who I am and that's all I want to be
I am sorry you are disappointed and my
greatness you fail to see
In the blink of an eye, you'll have me forget who
I am
but I'm rooted in authenticity and anything less
is a scam

Insecurity is calling, it knows me by name
Your ancient expectations are what's to blame
You thought I would change, become easier to
swallow—
a watered-down version of me
steeped in sorrow
But that can never be me,
I shine like the sun,
the moonlight is jealous of what I've become

Too much for some and not enough for others,
she's a mystery, a puzzle with too many layers to
discover

I won't let you define me, your schema I reject
I live my life full of light and with no regrets
No, I won't let you project your inadequacy onto me,
No, not today, that can never be.

Tolerate

In childhood's quiet, I learned to see,
Love's subtle dance of tolerating me.
My parents' love, often disguised,
Equating love where tolerance lies.
The baggage that I bring along,
Of childhood days where I didn't belong,
Shapes my fears and fuels my quest,
To love and give you my very best.

Now with you, I face this truth,
Our hearts are entwined, yet seeking proof.
You crave touch, where I need air,
To say I tolerate leads to despair.
When I said "tolerate," I meant to show,
A willingness to let love grow.
Stepping out of comfort zones,
To keep you near, to call you home.

In love's embrace, we often find,
A quiet place where our hearts aligned.
I want you near, through joy and strife,
In every second of this shared life.
For love is not a perfect tale,
It weathers storms but our love can prevail.

You cherish touch, I seek my space,
In love's vast, tender, shared embrace.
Sometimes I struggle, out of my zone,
To bridge the gap, so you're not alone.
I carry baggage from my youth,
In intimate moments when I don't mean to.
We're learning still, with each passing day,
To navigate love's intricate way.
And though at times, it's tough to see,
Your love is everything to me.

When the world feels much too loud,
I tolerate to make you smile
But what I meant, in truth, to say,
is that I'd choose you any day.
For love, at times, is compromise,
To see the world through each other's eyes
For meeting others where they stand,
is the purest love at hand.
Where compromise is a two-way street
With tolerance, your needs I hope to meet
Even when it's not what I need
The love I have for you intercedes.

In moments harsh, when I speak clear,
I find myself the villain here.
Yet tolerance, in love's own frame,
is meeting needs, not causing shame.

So why is tolerance viewed as less,
When compromise is love's caress?
For in our trials, we come to see,
That love's true strength is empathy.
Tolerate, to me, means more,
Than just enduring, as before.
It's choosing you, in every light,
Even when the words don't come out right.

Science

Science,
The literal art of fucking around and finding out.
Don't let this smile and grace fool you.
I shine so bright that the sun envies me,
But I can pop off if I need to.
You can try me if you want to.
A social experiment of sorts
To see how far you can push me.
That's cute, bless your heart.

Science can be so freeing,
Chemicals mix to find a perfect life balance
Or
Biology takes over, and neurotransmitters kick
into high gear.
Dopamine overriding oxytocin,
putting you in your place brings me joy.
Telling you about yourself, in multiple
languages is my gold star.
Ah, science.
So life-giving,
but so dangerous in the wrong hands.
Be careful,
I can hold space for both.

Sunrise on the Savannah

6 am wake-up calls and stretches reaching up to
the morning sky.
Half awake, a small, still voice echoes in my
mind
"You are chosen, for this moment, for this
purpose"
As we reach the top of the hill,
Warm tears stain my frozen cheeks as I stare in
awe.
I can feel God's love in the warmth of the sun.
Joy does come in the morning
Grand rising from the badimo-the ancestors
They awaken to help make dreams a reality,
and to reveal past wisdom.
Oranges and yellows paint the backdrop of
acacias that open like umbrellas to welcome the
day.
Dust-covered shoes and clear quartz guide our
path to full hearts and renewed spirits.
So much hope lives in the sunrise.
As long as the sun rises over the savannah,
I have hope.
Hope for a better me,
a better day,
a better world.

Reading material for sleep

Book nerds meet online
How did we get so lucky?
Love has smiled on us

Loves music, loves dance
My hips sway to your heartbeat
Your smile makes me melt

One-of-a-kind love
Once in a lifetime for sure
Way too rare for words

Rae of shining light
Creatrix, Intuitive soul
She a pure moonbeam

I am the muse, but
Our love is the masterpiece
Favorite canvas

Sit in your feelings
Standing in my own shit now
A beautiful mess

Love can be scary
Unexpected affection
Brain and heart battle

Pre-sleep chats abound
watch me sleep and hold me close
Polite snuggle texts

Melancholia,
becomes my middle name
Fake it, to make it

Love is torturous
Uncertainty looms throughout
Wild hearts can't be tamed

Broken hearts take shape
you say I never loved you
Oh, amnesia strikes

We can't be friends now
'Cause you closed the doors behind you
Only words are left

Be free; wanderlust

Eyes closed in the dark of night,
I hear a faint cry of a spirit asking, begging,
praying to be free.
The howl of the wind and drifting thoughts
respond, "Do you even know what it means to
be free?"
Maybe.
Maybe it's the light breeze of a Ghanaian
morning or hearing the waves crash off a coast
meant to enslave, meant to stifle, but then being
reminded that the Lion of Judah will always win.
Or it's holding on to the side of a boat in the
Indian Ocean and finally being brave enough to
let go, even for a second.
It's siestas with the window open, recharging in
the Ecuadorian sun, foreshadowing excursions
to Aztec ruins in the Yucatan.
Wide-eyed under the midnight sky, catcalls of
Black beauty and leftover fireworks crunching
beneath my feet.
Reminding me that I'm not actually floating.
It's the aroma of the spice market, the blaring of
rickshaw horns, or the taste of the finest Chai
India has to offer.

The dichotomy of the Taj Mahal against littered
streets.
My heart will always be the freest with chitenge
in tow and hips swaying to drums just as freeing
as two-stepping to 2nd lines in Congo Square.
Freedom is loving your body enough to hike
4-hour waterfalls, skinny dip in lakes, and be
showered by the mist of the Smoke That
Thunders.
The joy of chasing giraffes and petting lions.
The audacity to be Black in Africa.
The resiliency to be quirky, queer, and
quintessentially…me.
Why can't I feel free at home, happy but never
truly free?
Let this be your inspiration,
A declaration to live authentically.
Instead,
I let every ounce of me disappear behind the
shadows of my Smokies.
I melt back into a spineless puddle of
people-pleasing,
Projecting everything but 100% that bitch.
What would Lizzo do? (Snap and pivot)
What are the ancestors saying?
What is Creator feeling?
"I love you so, but if you don't, I have to
leave"...

Wanderlust brings me closer to you but further
from the norm
…. and that's freedom.

Lion tamer

I met him at sunset
His skin was as smooth as cocoa butter and his
eyes twinkled like the north star.
I was taken aback by the sweet smirk across his
lips.
I wasn't expecting to see a smile that could
match the marvel of the African night sky
He was suave, charming, and a boss in all
regards.
His lion totem makes perfect sense as the
conversation flows like wine.
Attentive, filling my glass and my mind with
full-bodied notes.
Casual conversations with others in the room
quickly turn into thoughts of us being alone.
Imagining what we could do in the warm glow
of a fire under the light of the moon.
One bottle of white wine later, I find myself
touching his back, his leg, his…
Heart? Probably not.
I've been around these types before
Love 'em and leave 'em, a whole ass family
waiting at home
But tonight, he's here.

Covering me with blankets, touching my back,
and moving his hand lower.
We decide it's best to depart.
Our commitments and responsibilities get in the
way and bring us back to reality
One last soft request as I ask him if he's ok.
Still with that twinkle in his eye,
I make him a pinky promise to be ok and we seal
it with a kiss.
I can't kiss his lips the way I long to but at least
my lips are touching some part of him.
As I turn to leave, I feel myself move nearer to
him
Is it gravity? Is my balance off? What is this
force?
It's the intoxication of his touch pulling me in
and the sweet heat from his lips pressed against
my neck.
Even the most ravenous of lions can be tamed by
the right lioness
But he leaves,
not mine to tame and not mine to hold for more
than a moment.
The vivid memories of his touch and the copious
glasses of wine make my head spin.
The night ends but the feeling lingers
and the urge to tame lions remains.

Homesick

Homesick for a place and a culture I don't know
Homesick for a love that's lost
Longing for a sense of self.
Authenticity is hard when you don't know where
you come from.
The feeling when you finish a good book
and long for more words to magically appear on
the page.
Homesick for a country that isn't mine,
a village that raised me,
Echos of children's laughter in the chill of cold
season.
Homesick for who I thought I was, for who I
thought you were,
Before reality hit us both.
Homesick for something that never existed but
always talked about.
Homesick for friends who love and see you
more than families of origin
Friends who feel like family and
feel like home.
Homesick for belly laughs, comedic tears, and
nostalgia latent theories with people whose
closeness transcends bloodlines.
Homesick for the reality I created for myself.

Botho: a call to action

I am because we are;
a declaration many won't understand,
a decree made by the "savage,"
the "uncivilized," the developing nation.
Community and collective work are foreign
concepts to capitalists,
especially when perception is everything.
We fear what we don't understand and trust no
one,
It's the way of the Western world.
But here,
I am because we are,
I am my sister's keeper.
I honor the Divine in you even when you
mistreat me.
A call to action for the world over.
To earn respect is to give respect,
no bullying tactics needed.
Break molds, and build bridges.
Be humble but know who you are.
Be your ancestors' wildest dreams while
breaking generational curses.
Love thy neighbor better than you love yourself,
because lack of self-love is the root of all evil.
How can I possibly hate you and love myself?

Botho,
People are people because of people.
We are the same,
we are the people,
we are the ones who can press the reset button,
I only hope we aren't too late.

Happy Poem

They told me to write a happy poem;
As if my feelings are one-dimensional.
I can feel immense joy but fail to find words to
give the feelings justice.
Longing is an easy emotion to write about,
It's a constant state.
Anger comes through better in the written word
because I know my words can be lethal.
Sadness is too predictable.
I rarely feel regret, I don't live my life that way.
So here's your happy poem,
I only write it to make you stay.

Imposter

Feeling all the feels,
Dreamstate appearances,
My ex, my parents, my new obsession.
The image of my childhood home as a
placeholder for approval that never came.

Always looking to others
For validation,
Never internal.
My sense of self is wavering,
Crumbling under the weight
Of side-eyes and words left unsaid.

Exes,
a source of more disapproving looks, and the
energy of regret.
The sting of "you're not my type" intensifies
with declarations of "I thought you'd change";
Only to be left with trauma-induced
compatibility.
Faking confidence but yearning for validation
The type of validation that only arrives
if I look and act the part;
meeting inexplicit criteria.

The urge to binge, I cannot surf.
It's the only thing to quiet the noise.
Being alone, having a choice, being perceived;
They all make the noise so much louder.

Surrounded by pleasantries and formalities
Without real concern.
I'm drowning, suffocating
Under the pressure to be…
Palatable, Beautiful,
Heard, and Significant— Everything I'm not.

So I remain an imposter.

In a field that doesn't celebrate me,
In a body that doesn't feel like mine,
In a society that pretends to care.
In a family that keeps secrets and casts shadows,
In the absence of belonging.

Growth is continual,
But who or what am I growing into?
Shadows of a being I don't know,
Yet everyone else seems to know so well.

Ready

I think I'm ready to try again,
The thing called love.
The social experiment of the heart.
I'm ready to hold hands, sometimes,
And cuddle and laugh until the wee hours of the
morning.
I think I'm ready to try again,
Giving my all to someone new.

I think I'm finally over the last love lost.
My first love,
the 12-months-and-19-days love.
The love that filled my heart with joy I didn't
think was possible
and also fueled a wrath I wouldn't wish on
anyone.

I think I'm ready.
To be open about who I am.
Open about the parts of myself that are shunned
by churches, governments, and family members
alike.
I think I'm ready, to be honest,
Honest about my past.

The past that happened in the shadows of bus
stops and family sleepovers gone wrong.
I think I'm ready to be me.
No more hiding behind fake smiles and funny
fat friend troupes.

I'm ready,
ready to let go of narratives that no longer serve
me.
Ready to reframe things and change my
perspective.
Ready to be…who I've always wanted to be,
Ready to embrace who I've always been.

Spirit

What science fails to explain
Spirit knows intuitively,
Intimately.
Written in the very fabric of time,
Etched in the stars of the African sky
and the orange and garnet hues of the Smoky
Mountains.
Spirit, God, Jah, Creator, Universe, Orishas—
all semantics;
But the feelings they evoke are the same.
The feeling I get when I simply touch the
Baobab tree.
The surge of emotions at seeing the sunrise
Every. Single. Morning.
I am constantly in awe and continuously
humbled that I get to breathe in this air.
Honored to travel to lands where I don't speak
the language yet still feel connected.
Reverence to feel a presence that is so much
bigger than me,
but encapsulates all that I can be.
Spirit, lead me.
A force that lives inside of me, that lives inside
of all of us.

A source of answers to questions I haven't even
begun to ask.
A sense of peace amidst chaos,
A stillness that garners peace that surpasses all
understanding yet does not feel stagnant.
A gratitude that no other words could express.
Spirit.

www.ingramcontent.com/pod-product-compliance
Lightning Source LLC
Chambersburg PA
CBHW071234140726
47996CB00007B/2607